The Cardinal *Mysteries*

A **WORKBOOK** to help you navigate your awakening.

HOPE *floats*™

LET IT IN.

Above all your earthly worries, hope floats.
All you need do is let it in.

ISBN-13: 978-0692985700 (Chewning Design, LLC)
ISBN-10: 0692985700

The
Cardinal
Mysteries

STEPHANIE C. CHEWNING

CONTENTS

WORKSHEETS

CONNECTING THE DOTS

Anyone who knows me well will tell you that I love cardinals. Cardinals are a somewhat common red bird in the eastern United States, where I live. The males are bright red and the females are a darker red brick color. In winter they stand out against the crisp white snow and are often found in holiday decor. I have always loved these red birds, but they took on a new meaning for me in 2006–2008 when I started to see them with unusual frequency.

My father had been diagnosed with an illness in 2006 that had taken my family down into the dizzying world of assisted living, nursing homes, and the healthcare system. We were making decisions, and then second-guessing ourselves as to what was best for my father. One day, while walking my dog, I looked to the sky and asked to be given a sign that we were making the right decisions.

Just then, a cardinal flew down and perched itself on the fence. I didn't know it then, but that was the beginning of an abundance of cardinals showing up in my life.

At the time I took it to be a sign. But as life has unfolded, I also see synchronicity as a beautiful example of how the Universal Laws play a role in our lives. *If you have ever wondered if there is a grand design to life, then you are reading the right book.* This book will help you to understand why you repeat certain patterns in your relationships, in your jobs, and in other areas such as health and finances. Everything is related; all you have to do is connect the dots to begin to understand.

This book may give you some of the answers that you are looking for, but others will remain for you to unravel on your own. You are about to start a journey of discovery and just as you solve one mystery, another invariably presents itself.

This is not a book on religion, but it will touch on *spirituality*. This is not a medical book, but it will touch on *healing*. This is not a science book, but it will touch on some principles of *energy*. I have come to learn that spirituality, healing, and science are all connected. Once you know the system we work in, you will see that it is a beautiful system. ~ *Stephanie Chewning*

There is something beyond the world that we see, hear, and touch.
There is a veil of perception that separates
us from a broader perspective.

PATTERNS

Over the years, I have noticed certain patterns repeating in my life and in the lives of those around me. A relationship would end and another would start with similar themes. I'd notice coincidences that didn't seem random—not necessarily important, but curious nonetheless. Perhaps you have also noticed certain patterns bubble up again and again in your own life.

What patterns do you see repeating in your life? Have you noticed patterns in relationships, patterns in jobs, patterns in health? *The pattern is the clue.*

So what forms these patterns? **It is your repeated thoughts and beliefs.** But let me first tell you about a part of the human structure that you may not be aware of, and it may be hard to comprehend at first. There is more to you than just the *physical* body. There is also an *energetic* aspect to you. Eastern medicine and philosophy is comfortable with this concept, but many in the West are not familiar (or comfortable) with this concept.

I have been aware of some aspects of Eastern philosophy since my art college years in the mid-1980s. This was a time when "New Age" thinking was gaining steam. I grew up with music that hinted at things I would later study: The Beatles' exploration of Indian spirituality and Transcendental Meditation. The Beach Boys singing about "good vibrations." There were hints of things that others knew, but I never considered their meaning.

> What patterns do you see repeating in your life? Have you noticed patterns in relationships, patterns in jobs, patterns in health?
>
> **The pattern is the clue.**

During college, small groups of artists would sometimes have interesting philosophical conversations in the late hours about exotic topics such as karma, reincarnation, psychics, and out-of-body experiences. It was fun and captivating but over the years my imagination didn't expand much beyond noticing the chakra posters hanging on the walls of a yoga studio. Those familiar illustrations, with seven colorful circles through the center of the body, were just wall art to me for many years.

While I was in college, I met a couple from California who introduced me to meditation. They told me that if I ever wanted to relax, I should just sit and count my breath—breathe in and silently count to three, and then exhale to five. It was simple and I would sometimes do that for 5–10 minutes if I was anxious about an exam.

In the years after college I would sometimes meditate as a way of managing the stress that came with the deadlines of the advertising world that I now worked in. But it was a <u>reactive</u> practice. In other words, I didn't meditate until <u>after</u> I was stressed about something. It was like taking an aspirin.

I don't remember exactly when I started to practice meditation more regularly, but it was in response to the growing stress in my life over my father's illness and other stresses in my life. In 2008 my father died, the economy had suddenly collapsed, I lost 75% of my clients in one week, and a romantic relationship had ended. It was a very difficult year. I found that following my breath for 20 minutes a day, a few times a week helped.

I continued this type of meditation for a few years. Then, in 2010, I started to meditate every day, twice a day, once upon waking and again in the evening. I usually meditated for 20–40 minutes at each sitting. Sometimes I would simply follow my breath. Other times I would say a word (mantra). My only intention was to calm myself and improve my health, which was deteriorating from years of high stress. *2010 was also the year I started to feel buzzy.*

Several times a week I would wake up around 3 a.m. thinking I was feeling the bed vibrate. The sensation would then run through my entire body. I thought some equipment in the storage room beneath my condo unit was making the room vibrate, but my repeated exploration of the storage room revealed nothing. It was not an uncomfortable buzzy feeling, but it was not subtle—it woke me up and lasted for hours.

> Once the energy is rebalanced, the body has an easier time healing. Most Reiki training, while not religious in nature, teaches spiritually-based emotional intelligence and empathy.

One day, I noticed the buzzy feeling while awake, during meditation: a vibrational sensation that started in my head then washed down into my body. This is when I realized the bed was not vibrating. I was.

I had taken enough yoga classes to be familiar with what is called Kundalini energy. So I scoured the internet looking for descriptions. A "Kundalini Awakening" didn't sound like what I was experiencing. My research told me that Kundalini rests in the <u>bottom</u> of the body and rises <u>*up*</u>, sometimes forcefully opening chakras along the way.

This energy that I was experiencing was gently flowing <u>*down*</u> from the head, and sometimes not even leaving the head. But I found what I needed to know at that time. Meditation can awaken the energetic centers (chakras) in the body and stimulate the glands associated with those chakras. The energy in my body was moving and I was now sensitive enough to feel the vibrational shift that was a result of the meditation I had been practicing. Years later there would be other shifts and chakra openings, but at that time I understood that my energy body was waking up.

REIKI

I continued to experience the buzzy feeling over the years that followed. I was no longer waking up at 3 a.m. but would often feel energy circulating through my body during the day. I became a voracious reader of anything that talked about energy, metaphysics, or other esoteric knowledge. Although the buzzing became less frequent as the years unfolded, my hands would often feel like they were in a bubble of static electricity with heat flowing through them and my body.

In 2014 I decided to take a Reiki class. I wasn't really sure what Reiki was, but knew it would cover the chakra system and talk about energy. I quietly took the Reiki class in hopes I would learn something about the energy field.

Reiki is a healing technique that was developed in Japan in the late nineteenth century. It is a simple technique for transferring healing energy to another person through hands-on and hands-off methods.

Reiki practitioners are often empathic and are trained to sense the energetic fields around the body, as well as detect and correct energy blockages. They don't actually flow *their* energy into you, but rather connect and direct the *universal energy* (which flows through everything) to <u>influence</u> the energy in your body. Once the energy is rebalanced, the body has an easier time healing. Most Reiki training, while not religious in nature, teaches spiritually-based emotional intelligence and empathy. (Healing Touch/Therapeutic Touch, found in hospitals, is another energy practice but is not taught with a spiritual basis.) I later went through the other levels of study to develop a full understanding of the techniques. My intention was not to practice or teach Reiki; it was only to understand what was happening to my body. Over the years I have added my own methods and expanded my understanding into what I simply call the *Principles of Energy*.

ENERGY

It has many names...Prana, Qi, Chi, Ki...but I simply refer to it as *Energy*. We are told that everything is energy, but what is energy? In science class we learn about types of energy—kinetic energy, thermal energy, electromagnetic energy, and atomic energy. Our bodies also flow with these energies. When the energy moves through me it feels buzzy and charged (electric). It has momentum (kinetic), it feels like heat at times (thermal), and it feels like it flows through me at every level (atomic). It also feels like there is a consciousness involved that can be directed.

Science tells us that electricity and magnetics go hand in hand, and that everything vibrates at the atomic level. The negatively charged electrons orbit around the center of the atom, with centrifugal force pulling away from the center. The positively charged protons (next to the neutrally charged neutrons) at the center are pulling the electrons in. This push-pull energy creates a vibrational wave pattern at this tiny level of our existence involving magnetics and electricity.

We are electromagnetic beings. If you've ever had an MRI, they were working with the magnetic properties of the hydrogen atoms that make up the water in your body. If you've ever had an EEG or an EKG they were measuring the electrical activity of your brain or heart. So when we talk about our vibration and frequency, it will help to remember that we are vibrational and electromagnetic.

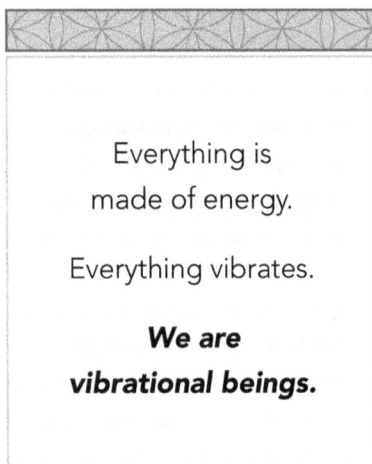

> Everything is made of energy.
>
> Everything vibrates.
>
> **We are vibrational beings.**

VIBRATION AND FREQUENCY

Perhaps you have heard someone talk about raising their frequency, or increasing their vibration. But what does this mean? I think it is an attempt to explain a complex law of physics that we do not fully understand yet (or at least I don't). In ancient mystical teachings there are *Universal Laws*. The *Law of Vibration* states that everything that exists is energy, which vibrates at a particular frequency.

Vibration is a wave-like movement. Remember that everything vibrates at the atomic level. A push-pull energy between an atom's orbiting electrons and its nucleus is always at play. Everything is made of energy. Everything vibrates. We are vibrational beings.

Frequency is a measure of oscillation. It is a measurement of how often something happens within a measurement of time. For example, the frequency of a brainwave is how many times the sine wave cycles back and forth in a second. We are electromagnetic beings with various frequencies (depending upon what is being measured...the brain, organs, or atoms).

When we experience a lower emotion like fear or anger, it is an indicator that the <u>thought</u> that triggered the emotion is putting stress on the system and our overall frequency gets suppressed. We vibrate at a lower speed. We produce less energy (or perhaps a different energy). This energy feeds our body. We understand that we need water and nourishment for a healthy body, but we also need energy.

When we focus on thoughts that trigger emotions like joy, love, or appreciation, this returns us to the higher frequencies the body thrives on. When we start to raise our frequency, we may become sensitive to that vibrational shift, especially if it is a dramatic shift. I believe this is the buzzy feeling I experienced in 2010. I was feeling my cells, or their atoms, vibrating at a higher speed than I was used to. I still occasionally experience that buzzing, as I continue to raise my frequency.

Emotions on the lower end of the scale (anger, jealousy, hatred) do not feel good to us. They may capture our attention; we may even find interest in the drama of a situation— but if you notice how the body feels, **it does not feel good.**

These emotions are stressful to the body.

ENERGY MERIDIANS

Our structure is a complex mechanism bridging the *physical* body with the *energetic* body. Eastern medicine is based on the principle that seven main energetic meridians (chakras) govern the physical body. Each meridian is associated with a gland, and each gland governs particular organs. (We also have additional chakras above and below the body that connect us to the Earth and to the Universe.)

Our emotions can often be felt in certain areas of the body. For example, if you are nervous about public speaking and you are on stage in front of an audience you might feel a tightening in the throat. This is a physical manifestation of the energy meridian located in the throat area starting to constrict. Energy does not easily flow to the throat during this situation. It is a common occurrence, and not of concern in the short term. But imagine if you've spent a lifetime not speaking up for yourself, feeling fear about voicing your opinions, or not feeling like you could speak your truth. Over a prolonged period of time, the restriction of this meridian may not nourish the thyroid gland or the organs that it governs.

The body has seven main meridians and many more smaller meridians that regulate energetic flow. If we experience physical fear, we often say that we feel a "knot" in our stomach. If we experience sadness due to death or grief, we might feel tightness in the chest. These are examples of how our emotions indicate the energetic flow in our lower meridians or our heart meridian. Again, not an issue in the short term, but repeated daily over a long period of time these emotions can manifest physically in the body. The cellular vibrational frequency in that area of the body becomes affected. The energy does not freely flow to nourish the cells, resulting in pain or illness.

Emotions on the lower end of the scale (anger, jealousy, hatred) do not feel good to us. They may capture our attention; we may even find interest in the drama of a situation—but if you notice how the body *feels*, it does not feel good. The thoughts that bring on these emotions are stressful to the body.

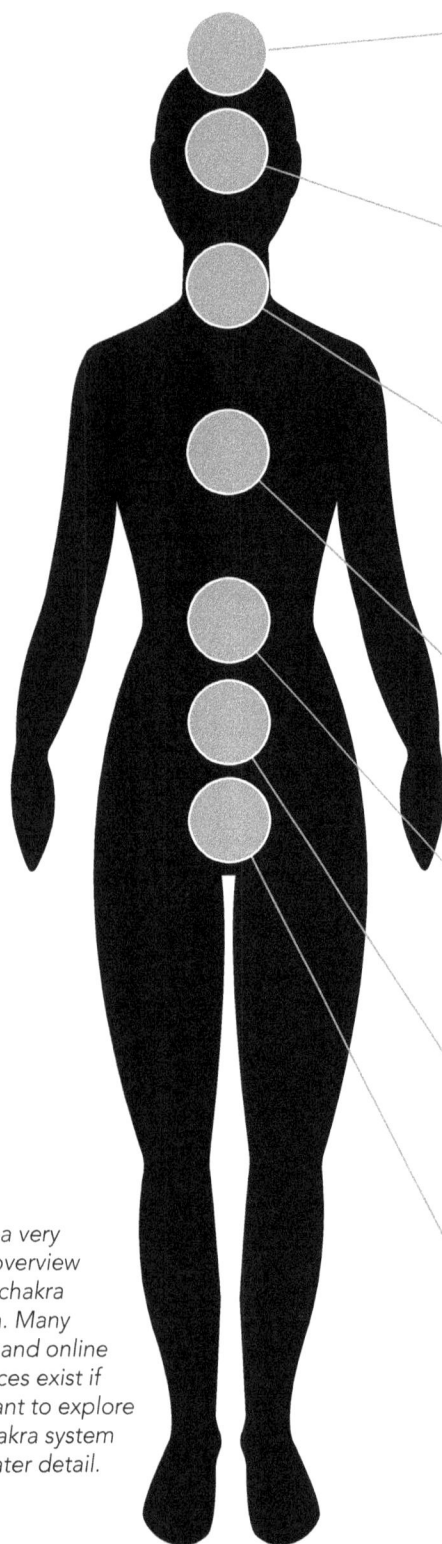

● **CROWN CHAKRA** *(associated with the color* **violet***)*
Top of the head, where the fontanel is on an infant

Pineal Gland: upper brain, right eye, muscular system, skeletal system, skin

Associated with consciousness and enlightenment

● **BROW CHAKRA** *(associated with the color* **indigo***)*
Forehead, between or above eyebrows

Pituitary Gland: lower brain, left eye, ears, nose, nervous system

Associated with spiritual wisdom, inner vision, and intuition

● **THROAT CHAKRA** *(associated with the color* **blue***)*
At the throat, the area of the Adam's apple notch

Thyroid: lungs, trachea, esophagus, neck vertebrae, mouth, teeth and gums, vocal chords

Associated with communication, self-expression, creativity, and judgment (of self and others)

● **HEART CHAKRA** *(associated with the color* **green***)*
Center of the chest

Thymus: heart, blood, Vagus nerve, circulatory system, shoulders and arms, ribs, breasts, upper back, diaphragm

Associated with unconditional love and compassion

● **SOLAR PLEXUS CHAKRA** *(associated with the color* **yellow***) Just above the navel*

Pancreas/Spleen: stomach, liver, gallbladder, nervous system, intestines, middle back

Associated with emotion (positive/negative), personal power

● **SACRAL CHAKRA** *(associated with the color* **orange***)*
Just below the navel

Gonads: reproductive system, bladder, lower back, large intestine, pelvis, hips, appendix

Associated with pleasure, desire, sexuality, creativity

● **ROOT CHAKRA** *(associated with the color* **red***)*
Tailbone/Perineum

Adrenals: spinal column, kidneys, bones, legs

Associated with physical survival, financial survival, family support

This is a very basic overview of the chakra system. Many books and online resources exist if you want to explore the chakra system in greater detail.

The emotions on the higher end of the scale (joy, love, appreciation) feel good to us. This is the healing frequency for the body.

Often, when people start to meditate or focus on their thoughts, they evolve to a new level of emotional thinking. Studies have shown that meditation changes brain wave patterns. People who meditate often say that they notice that meditation changes the way they think and feel. They move up the emotional scale from fear and anger to love and empathy. They begin to think more clearly. They are less reactive to negative stimuli. They are "the calm in the storm." Meditation naturally will raise your frequency because as you stop thought (or quiet the mind for short periods of time) you stop the stressful thoughts that are bringing down the vibratory frequency of your body. As you raise your frequency, you may actually feel the energy moving and adjusting like I did. But not everyone will translate energy in this way, so don't be discouraged if you don't. You will translate energy in ways that are right for you.

The physical importance of maintaining our frequency and vibration is health. There are many things that affect vibration in addition to our thoughts...food, water, nature, sound, light, and other frequencies in our environment (natural and man-made) just to name a few. But there is also an experiential aspect of vibrational frequency.

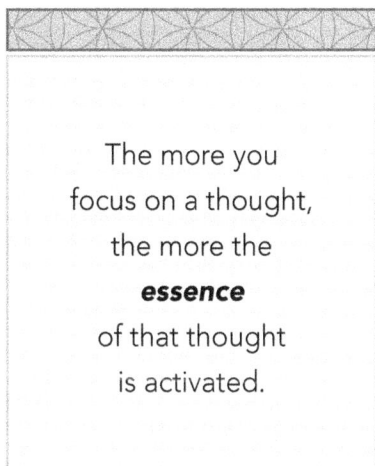

CREATIVE LAW

> The more you focus on a thought, the more the
> ***essence***
> of that thought is activated.

We are *spiritual* beings having a *physical* experience. We are also *creative* beings. We attract people, things, and experiences into our lives through the repeated thoughts that we think. We broadcast the frequency of that thought out into the world. The thought doesn't always translate specifically, but it is like saying, "Bring to me the essence of this thing that I am now focusing on."

When you **focus on a thought**, positive or negative, the vibration of that thought becomes active. It is a signal going out into the world looking for people, things, and opportunities to match it. The more you think a thought, the more dominant that vibration becomes. Dominant vibrational thoughts pick up momentum and become more "material." The more that materializes around those thoughts, the more those thoughts become **beliefs**. It is a feedback loop of self-fulfilling beliefs. What you believe becomes your truth.

Our **emotions** are our guidance system. We are meant to experience joy. If we are experiencing a negative emotion around a thought, it tells us that we have gone off course from what will truly make us happy. That is the time to pivot your thoughts into a more positive direction. Many of us do this naturally when we look for the "silver lining" in a situation. Emotions do not fuel manifestation, but are an indicator of direction and momentum (how fast it will manifest). Strong negative emotion tells us that we are not only off course but picking up speed. Positive emotion tells us we are on track. When I saw that first cardinal, I thought it was a sign so I focused on them even more. I now have years of momentum around cardinals and I don't actively focus on them other than to **appreciate** them when I see them and I continue to manifest them almost daily. It's a feedback loop and the system likes repetitive patterns. What pattern of thought do you repeat on a regular basis? If you like what is manifesting in your life, continue to appreciate it. If you don't like what is manifesting in your life, stop focusing on it and break the feedback loop. If you are experiencing something difficult, you aren't being punished by God. You simply focused on something for too long and got caught in the feedback loop. It's time to pivot into positive thoughts. Can you find a truly positive aspect to what you are experiencing? If so, let that be your new focus. It will start to shift the energy.

If you are new to *Creative Law* you may have a hard time believing these things. Remain open-minded. Don't believe it because I, or someone else, tells you about it. Let it unfold in your life like it did for me with the cardinals. Be intentional and ask to be shown examples. Look for patterns and synchronicities that you see repeating. Examine your thoughts and beliefs to see if there are connections to what materializes in your life. Have fun with it. It is a beautiful system of creation when you understand how it works.

> **Like attracts like.**
>
> More coincidences and synchronicities are experienced when deliberate thought is practiced.

This *Creative Law* is commonly referred to as *The Law of Attraction*. Like attracts like. This explains why more coincidences and synchronicities are experienced when deliberate thought is practiced.

I'll share with you some principles of how it works later in this workbook, but don't over-think it. You don't have to be a master mechanic to be a great driver. **If all you take away from this workbook is to learn to pivot into better-feeling thoughts, you'll be fine.** If you want to learn more, read on. Be open-minded, and if all that follows does not resonate with you, hang on to what makes sense and leave the rest to ponder for another time. Someday you may believe in things that you do not believe in now. It is brave to question reality. But go gently—not everyone is ready to awaken to reality.

QUICKENING

Scientists are telling us that electromagnetic conditions on our planet are changing. Could these changes also affect human frequencies? Are solar and cosmic activity transitioning us into new energy patterns that are affecting our bodies and brains? If these changes are affecting our frequencies, as I suspect they are, then learning to raise our frequencies through deliberate positive focus will be beneficial. If we are positively focused, we will adapt to these changes more easily. People who are focused in lower emotions will find these times more challenging. Many teachers are stepping forward to help the Earth's population during this time of shift.

I believe that this system of creation was designed for us to manifest faster as we evolve and understand our creative abilities. At lower frequencies we are like children learning to ride a bike. We wanted to experience lower emotion, to have a full understanding of the duality of life. At lower frequencies, the manifestations were slower, allowing us to feel the negative emotion and then shift up the emotional scale before we created. In this "quickening" time, the frequencies are rising and the training wheels are being removed as manifestations are coming faster.

A TIME OF AWAKENING

Don't fear this higher frequency, because it also opens the doors to expanded consciousness. With that expanded knowledge we will learn to manifest at faster speeds, but through compassion. In other words, we are taking the first baby steps in our own evolution.

Many Reiki practitioners and Energy workers believe that the frequency of the human body is calibrated to the Earth. If Earth's frequency is changing, how is this affecting our own frequency and nervous system? Are we being influenced into a higher vibrational frequency? Energy workers and those in the spiritual communities are calling this the "*Time of Awakening.*" It is my belief that we are all being influenced into higher vibratory rates and these changes affect people differently. For people who are not resisting these shifts, they lift their vibration. They then experience higher levels of thinking (consciousness, enlightenment) with greater compassion. They *awaken* to truth. (They read books like this.) But for people who are resisting these shifts, they are put into states of agitation, illness, anger, and warring. A polarized society becomes more evident.

The mainstream public may not yet be open to these teachings, so I step into this with a bit of trepidation. But the stakes are too high to stay silent. These are not new teachings. They have been taught by spiritual teachers through the ages. They told us a shift was coming, and it is now here.

This system in which we live is based on love and compassion. It only stands to reason that we would expand our gifts through an expansion of the heart. The energy is shifting; frequencies are changing. The things we are focusing on are manifesting faster. Lower frequencies are being pushed to the surface and becoming more evident because they are not in tune with the new Earth frequencies. Negative things will continue to be in our world as long as the population remains negatively focused—but if we choose to focus on the positive end of the spectrum, we improve our chances of weathering the storm.

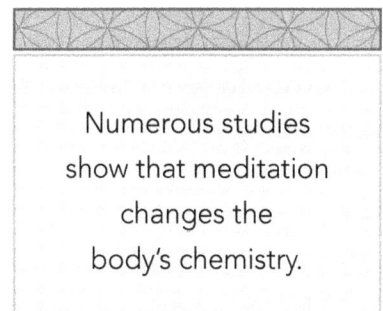

> Numerous studies show that meditation changes the body's chemistry.

As we are raised into higher frequencies, the lower frequencies in our lives are being pushed to the surface for us to recognize and clear. Does the violence in our world mirror the violence we watch on TV? Do the wars on the planet reflect the warring in our own personal lives? Does the anger in our politics mirror the anger in our homes or jobs? Earth's frequencies are affecting us, but our frequencies also affect Earth. Millenniums of human negativity were absorbed into her energy. Are hurricanes, earthquakes, and other natural geologic processes a way for Earth to release older, denser energies created by the human collective as Earth transitions to a higher frequency?

This is my best effort at explaining why raising our frequency is so important during this time. We must be intentional during the shift. Raising our vibratory rate will help us align with better health, become more compassionate, and survive as a species.

MEDITATION

When we meditate, we quiet the mind and are not focused on resistant negative thoughts. This allows our vibrational frequency to go where it naturally wants to go—up. It is so amazing to me that something as simple as quieting the mind can have such a profound affect on our health. Much of this can be explained by chemical changes in the body and brain when we slow down the breath during meditation.

Numerous studies show that meditation changes the body's chemistry. Stress hormones such as Cortisol and Adrenalin are reduced. Increased Endorphin levels can have an opiate effect that reduces pain. Increases in Serotonin levels can act as a mood elevator and may help fight cancer. Meditation can increase Oxytocin (the "love hormone") and increases in Melatonin, caused by meditation, may help with sleep. Increases in Human Growth Hormone (HGH) aid in healing. These are just a few well-documented examples of the benefits of meditation.

Brainwave patterns can also change during and after meditation. Depending upon how deep the meditation, brainwave patterns can even replicate the brainwaves seen during the various stages of sleep. Studies have also shown that meditation can help with the brain's neuroplasticity, affecting impulse control, behavioral changes, and increasing feelings of love, joy, and compassion.

SPIRITUAL GIFTS

I've tried to explain the topic of energy through science, but there is a non-physical aspect to it that is harder to explain. I'd like to step out of the box for a moment and talk about how we each individually work with energy.

Like snowflakes, no two people are energetically alike. Some people, when their vibrational frequency is raised, will start to move energy. Meridians clear and energy flows through the body, sometimes moving the body spontaneously. Sometimes people have transformative experiences. They start to see energy, or hear frequencies. Often these experiences open the person to what are sometimes referred to as "spiritual gifts."

> I believe at some level we are all **lightworkers**. Simply shine your light through example, by being compassionate and kind to your fellow human beings.

We all have a primary channel that we translate energy through. For example, someone who translates energy through sensation may <u>feel</u> energy as heat or tingling energy. A person who translates energy visually may <u>see</u> energetic patterns around people, animals, and things (auras). Some may translate frequencies as sound. In this new higher frequency, there are people who are spontaneously experiencing energy in ways they never did before. In mystical traditions, initiates were taken under the wing of a master who could guide them through those changes. But to the uninitiated, these spiritual gifts may be frightening, or at the very least confusing, if they are not understood.

When one energetic channel is saturated, another channel may open, adding additional abilities. There are many on the planet that chose to awaken at this time. To lead the way and to shine the light on the path. They are often referred to as *Lightworkers*. I believe at some level we are all lightworkers. You don't have to be a visionary, write a book, or be a healer. You can simply shine your light through example by being compassionate and kind to your fellow human beings. Not all will awaken at this time but everyone on the planet <u>chose</u> to experience this shift, and all have an opportunity to evolve to a new level of awareness.

FOCUS

Many people are awakening to the idea that there is more to this reality. Your Higher Self—that part of you that is connected to God, Source, Spirit, or whatever label you want to use—knows what is going on. You chose to come during this very special time. The frequency of the planet is rising, and we are rising along with it. *If we don't master the focus of our thoughts, we are in for a bumpy ride.*

There is an old saying: "Energy flows where the mind goes." The importance of where we focus our mind cannot be overstated. It's all a matter of airtime. How much time do you spend focusing on the negative things in your life, and how much time do you spend focusing on the positive things in your life?

You are surrounded by an electromagnetic bubble that emanates from all of your energy meridians. Your heart has the largest electromagnetic field in the body. It can be measured by equipment as far as 6 feet away from the body (and the field probably extends much further). Every time your heart beats, it pulses information throughout the body, saturating the tissues and organs, and cascading through every cell. But every heartbeat also pulses out into that energetic field that surrounds the body. The heart meridian is a broadcast mechanism reaching inward and outward, a two-way information portal that reacts to your focus and emotions.

Imagine a little mouse in a big meadow. Its heart field is expanding beyond its body, searching for food and sensing for danger. The mouse becomes aware of a cat. In fear, the mouse contracts its heart space so that it cannot be detected. This is how fear and negative emotion work in our bodies. For short amounts of time it is a good thing. It is a survival mechanism. But if we experience fear or other lower-frequency emotions for extended periods of time, it cuts off the vital flow of energy that nourishes the body. Fear and other negative emotions are necessary in a survival situation, but how often do you unnecessarily focus on thoughts that trigger negative emotion?

We all hold a mixture of beliefs, opinions, and expectations on a variety of subjects. As mentioned earlier, when you focus your attention on something, that vibration becomes activated and moves to the forefront. The more often you focus on it, the more dominant it becomes. **The emotions that accompany your thoughts serve as a navigation system.** If a thought creates an emotion that feels bad, it is telling you that you are off-track and that it is time to correct course by thinking a new thought. It is your free choice as a creator to determine where to put your focus. In that moment, you have the option of making a positive aspect of a situation dominant in your vibration or of making a negative aspect dominant.

> If we don't master
> our thoughts,
> we are in for a
> bumpy ride.
>
> **The importance of where
> we focus our mind
> cannot be overstated.**

It's a beautiful feedback system that was really meant to be quite simplistic: *If you think a thought that doesn't feel good, find a thought that feels better because you are going to attract the essence of that thought.* You don't have control over the details of how things show up in your life, but if you are focused on something that excites you (or annoys you), you will attract things to you that continue that theme of excitement (or annoyance) until you purposely change your focus or get distracted.

Imagine something you would like to experience. Your body has a positive emotional response, which lets you know that it is a thought that is beneficial. You are an energetic collection of every thought that you have ever thought. Unimaginable frequencies, intertwined and uniquely *you*. The more you focus upon this new thought, the more activated it becomes and it starts to manifest.

I can't explain how those things are drawn back to us or how the universe knows what to choose (I have become very comfortable with having faith in the unknowable). But I know from experience that what manifests is often beyond anything I could have known or imagined. We have limited view. God-Source energy flows through *everything*; it sees all cooperative components (which we are often unaware of). I don't understand it, but I have faith in its mastery.

THE COLLECTIVE

We are singular beings but we are part of the human collective. We manifest individually, but we also manifest collectively as a unified consciousness. We are all connected.

I'm sure as a collective, the human race has learned everything there is to learn about sorrow. We are now taking the first step toward evolving out of this phase of our existence. We've exhausted negativity. It's time to explore compassion and global unity. If you want to put it in spiritual terms, it is time to turn away from the dark and explore the light. But there's always free will and for those who wish to continue to explore the dark, they are free to make that choice. But for those of us who are awakening, we are drawn to the light like a moth to a flame. We are splitting off into two human collectives. So the question is, in what direction do you choose to focus? Do you want to be awake or stay asleep?

DIVINE BLUEPRINT (LIFE'S PURPOSE)

People sometimes feel that they have a specific calling in life, a life's purpose. I believe that we all have a "framework of intentions" when we are born. For most, it is very general blueprint. For example, one intention might be to be an *uplifter* (someone who brings happiness to the planet to help raise the frequency during the Shift). For some it is very specific like working with children. Through free will they can explore that theme in any way they choose (as a parent, a teacher, a pediatrician, a sports coach, etc.) Many are on the planet during this time with the specific intention of teaching the true nature of reality and doing it in their own personal way (lightworkers, ministers, channelers). Others have chosen to be healers and may have chosen traditional health careers (doctors, nurses) or unconventional paths (Reiki, acupuncture, intuitive healers). Some are here to create change (environmentalism, social justice). Others are here to break existing systems (financial, healthcare) so that others (visionaries) can rebuild those systems so that they align better with the new energy. If you are

> What are you passionate about or what gives you joy?
>
> **These are clues to your Life's Purpose.**

negatively triggered by a subject, but do not feel that it is part of your Life's Purpose, your focus may be adding to the negative energy of that problem. But if you are inspired to action and aligned with the solution (and not just complaining), you may have found your purpose. We are programmed to recognize our own "directives" through our interests and emotions. What inspires you? What do you spend hours reading up on or studying? What are you passionate about or what gives you joy? These are all clues to your Life's Purpose.

KARMA AND SOUL CONTRACTS

I don't view Karma as punishment for the wrongs that we did in another life or rewards for our good deeds. There is a cause and effect aspect, but I see it rather as a continuation of energies, a continuation of the learning process. What themes were you exploring in another life that weren't completed? For example, you may have explored themes of betrayal, abandonment, or heartbreak in another lifetime. If you didn't work through those lessons, you may get another chance to resolve (heal) those themes in this lifetime. Our energy bodies can also carry over strong karmic ties to physical health issues. A stabbing in another life may leave pain in that area in this lifetime until it is cleared. The good news is, in this new energy, those karmic ties are dissolving.

From a higher perspective we see all possibilities. We know that we will have the opportunity and ability to heal any issues. From that perspective our intention is primarily to expand our awareness, but not always to create a comfortable life. We may choose a difficult path that will provide catalysts for powerful lessons. These can be difficult lives with contracts that involve family members, lovers, and friends. But they are always meant to be clarifying experiences.

DARK NIGHT OF THE SOUL

Things are not always easy in a time of awakening. Shifting energies are pushing things to the surface to heal. Vibrational frequencies are changing and some people, places, and things that you attracted into your life at a lower frequency may no longer be a match as you shift up in frequency. People, places, and things may change or fall away to make room for something new. Change can be scary. Times may seem dark and full of sadness, but bit by bit things will improve. You may start to meditate, change your diet, or become more aware of the power of your thoughts. These and other changes will continue to raise your frequency. You will start to attract new people and experiences that better match your higher vibration. Don't get caught up in the negativity of the past or it will keep you in pain. Be brave and move forward with hope in your heart.

CONCLUSION

However "weird" any of this may sound, I hope you will be open-minded and consider the possibility that these teachings may be true. Do you see patterns in your life that connect to repetitive thoughts? If anything you have read in these pages resonates with you, then read ahead. The rest of this workbook has been designed to help you raise your frequency. I share some favorite processes and techniques. Have fun with them. Explore the mind and enjoy the inner journey.

PRINCIPLES OF ENERGY, AT A GLANCE

This section gives you some basics on how energy works in our lives.

Law of Attraction: Thoughts carry a vibration, and vibrational frequencies attract other like frequencies (the adage of "like attracts like"). Potential timelines exist that are both singular and collective in nature. We are all connected to a grid of consciousness that expands beyond our individual experience. If you think a thought, and continue to focus on that thought it will start to collect similar energies around it, and it will manifest in some way or another. It may take minutes, hours, days, or years to finally manifest <u>physically</u> in our reality...but the components begin lining up in the non-physical realm within less than a minute of that original focused thought. Level of desire, divine timing, rate of frequency, and momentum control the timing of manifestation.

Desire, Allowing, and Inspired Action: These are the three steps to manifesting. You experience a situation that brings you into an awareness of something that you want. A <u>*desire*</u> is launched into that Universal grid of consciousness. In a state of <u>*allowing*</u>, you have faith (belief) that the Universe is lining up all cooperative components. When the timing is right, you or another will be inspired into action that will bring this experience into reality. What trips us up is focusing on the lack of it materializing (Where's my money? Where's my lover? Where's my new job?). If it is a big desire, we often focus on the fear of not having it (What if I can't pay this bill? What if I am alone forever? What if I can't find a job?). And this also slows things down or attracts the opposite of what we want (because we are actually vibrating on the <u>opposite</u> end of the desire).

Polarity/Duality: We came to experience a world of duality. Everything has its opposite: positive and negative, abundance and lack, male and female, good and bad, love and hate, peace and war. When we explore a subject, we have the free choice to explore either end of that duality (positive or negative). If you want to explore the subject of money you can focus on the lack of money (and experience that reality) or you can focus on abundance (and experience that reality). We were meant to experience joy, but we have free will to experience the opposite of joy. All experiences, even those we define as "negative", are added to our collective understanding and are considered beneficial from a broader perspective.

Desire can overcome vibration: Strong desire (indicated by strong emotion) can overcome vibration. Sometimes referred to as a quantum leap, a strong desire can catapult you into a manifestation before things have lined up. Example: You have a strong desire to lose weight, but you aren't vibrationally lined up to do it in a healthy way. You aren't lovingly feeding your body nutritious food. You aren't lovingly giving your body the exercise it wants. You hate your reflection and are desperate to lose weight. It would be better to line up with the energy and lose the weight in a healthy way, but the strong desire trumps the vibrational alignment so it manifests as an illness that results in weight loss.

Path of Least Resistance: The Universe is conservative; it moves energy in the most efficient way possible. It finds the path of least resistance. When you focus on a very specific way for something to unfold, it slows down the manifestation. Focus on abundance, not winning the lottery. The lottery may be fun...but it may not be the most efficient way to bring you abundance. Focus on the qualities you want in a partner; focusing on a specific person may block the best match for your desires.

Continuation of Energy: Energy is neither created nor destroyed; it just changes form. When we sleep, there is no negative resistant thought so our vibrational frequency rises. When we wake, it returns to where it was when we went to sleep. This establishes a consistency in our reality. There is a similar continuation of energy from lifetime to lifetime. A person with a strong energy around music may be born into their next life with great musical ability. A person with strong energetic momentum around an unresolved issue may carry that into the next life to "heal." From a broader perspective, we understand that we are creators with the ability to focus thought and change reality. From that broader perspective we may choose a dysfunctional family, or a body with the genetic propensity for a disease. That illness is often like a seed that could remain dormant if not provided the energy (a low emotional frequency) to bring it into fruition. From a broader perspective, we know that illness can be a powerful catalyst that awakens us and brings us into greater awareness. Although admittedly, this is hard to fully accept when dealing with an illness.

HELPFUL TIPS

If you are overwhelmed by information, these tips will help you navigate everyday life.

Belief and Hope: Learning to shift into <u>belief</u> is often a difficult process, and for many it is a major stumbling block to experiencing a happier life. Can you fully <u>believe</u> that you will be pointed toward the right people, places, and opportunities that will fulfill your desires? Belief leads to awareness. If you don't believe, you will not see the opportunities as they present themselves to you. Belief is faith, and it is said that faith will set you free. If you stumble on belief, *hope* is a good fallback. Often, hope evolves into *belief*. If you are in illness or pain, there is a big energetic difference between experiencing illness in hope rather than in anger or fear. Can you feel hopeful while in pain? Can you feel hopeful with a diagnosis in your hand? There is also a difference in the body's chemical response. Anger and fear trigger stress hormones that make pain worse and suppress the immune system. Hope and other positive emotions stimulate the production of chemistry in the body that help with pain, and at the same time boost mood and immunity. This is why meditation is a helpful component in the healing process.

Break the Habit of Negativity: Are you a naturally positive or negative person? Are you always looking for the silver lining or waiting for the other shoe to drop? Are you attracted to positive people or are you attracted to drama and gossip? Are you a complainer? Turning away from the "small negatives" will build resiliency for when you have to deal with the "big negatives." It may mean developing a level of diplomacy the next time a friend wants to tell you how horrible

the world is. Some will not like your positive personality because misery loves company. Telling someone who just lost his or her job to "stay positive" may not go over well, but you can still be supportive and compassionate without getting pulled into a discussion on how bad the economy is. For now, that may be their reality to experience, it doesn't have to be yours.

TV and Social Media: Television and social media occupy much of our free time. What are you letting in? How do you feel when you watch the news? Are you in anger or fear? If so, turn it off. Are you drawn to "Reality TV" where everyone is fighting? Notice if it mirrors fighting and conflict in your own life. Do you easily gravitate to the latest negative discussions on social media around politics, healthcare, or other current social debates, or do you get distracted by yummy recipes and cute animal videos that pop up in your stream? I'm not advocating a head-in-the-sand approach, but are you adding your energy to solutions or to problems? It might mean getting off of social media for a while. It might mean turning off the TV or being selective about the movies and shows that you do watch. Can you be hopeful despite the facts presented on the nightly news? Can you imagine that there are positive things that are not being reported? As you shift to a more positive focus, the *Law of Attraction* will bring you more examples of positive change in the world and things won't seem so bleak. There will still be negative events in the world, but you will gravitate to solutions that others may not be seeing.

Become More Playful: Some adults are so serious (myself included) that it is hard to remember what it was like to be a child, without worries. Can you remember what it felt like to play all day? For most of us there were no worries about working, money, or health when we were children. Can you reconnect with your inner child and be playful again? Playfulness is a high vibration, and who doesn't like to have fun!

Food and Water: We know that what we eat and what we drink impacts the body profoundly. But the mainstream public does not understand that foods and liquids, even water, also have a frequency. As you raise your frequency, lower vibrational foods that you used to tolerate may no longer agree with you. Your body may no longer be a match for chemical additives, unnatural preservatives, or some genetically modified foods. Trust your instincts to draw you to foods that will benefit you most. Don't be surprised if you are inspired to try new diets or adopt better eating habits. Don't criticize your body for being sensitive or having allergies. Often those intolerances are blocking foods that do not serve you. And if you do eat something that you know is lower vibrational (but is oh so yummy), enjoy it. Savor it. Thank the body for allowing you that indulgence. There is a big difference between eating a donut in appreciation and eating one and later blaming, shaming, or hating yourself for the indulgence.

Water is of great importance. The new vibrational frequencies on Earth are shaking things up for us on both the energetic and cellular level. Drinking pure clean water will help flush dense energies and toxins that are being released and might otherwise get lodged in our tissues.

Meditation: Due to changes on our planet, our frequency is increasing, whether we know it or not. We are therefore manifesting faster. Meditation is being stressed as a way to counteract these vibrational shifts because most of us still have not mastered our thoughts. Twenty minutes, once or twice a day, is helpful. Don't like to meditate? Then find something that has the same effect. Find a sport that you love, practice yoga or a moving meditation like Tai Chi or Qigong, take a dance class, explore a creative art form, read something that expands the mind, watch the clouds—anything that is creative, brings you joy, or that disconnects you from negative emotion. If you can't find excitement or joy, look for some form of relief.

Appreciation: Can you find things to appreciate every day? Each morning before you get out of bed, think of 5–10 things to genuinely appreciate. They can be small things like the comfort of your pillow or the flowers you see by your window. This simple practice will help you line up the energy for the rest of your day, bringing you other things to appreciate. When you see things to appreciate during the day, quietly acknowledge them (think, "I see you, I appreciate you, thank you," or similar thoughts in your mind. No one else has to know your inner dialogue). The same practice at night will continue to help you fine-tune your frequency.

Nature: A great way to get in tune with Earth's new frequency is to walk in nature, set your feet on her dirt, touch her trees and rocks, and appreciate her plants and flowers. She will literally recharge you if you let her. So spend an hour or two outside each day if possible.

PERSONAL DISCERNMENT

So, you've made it through the foundational information, and now comes the nitty-gritty of how to raise your frequency in these changing times. This workbook is meant to drill down on the specifics of your *thought patterns*, but I do touch on other areas that interest me. If you wish to study these other topics in more detail, I will leave it to other teachers to tell you about their specific areas of expertise. My area of interest is giving an overview of how the Universe works (connecting the dots) and uncovering thought patterns that you may not be aware of and that do not serve you. At some point, we all need a little de-programming.

I suggest developing a level of *personal discernment* while you are on this journey. By this I mean trusting your gut. When you listen to someone, myself included, do they resonate with you? When you read something, does it "feel right?" There are many teachers during this time of awakening. People come from different religions, different educational backgrounds, speaking different languages, and having different interests. There are teachers coming forth with very diverse backgrounds and different teaching styles. Some teach through traditional religious explanations, some are more metaphysical; some connect to the angelic realm, and others their galactic families. Don't be in judgment of what others believe. There are teachers for all. Find the ones who resonate with you the most.

That being said, there are teachers that do not resonate with me. Everyone can have an off day and sometimes that's all it is. But also be aware that there are teachers that are here to teach at a lower-vibrational level, and teachers that are meant to teach at a higher-vibrational level. If something feels off to you, it probably isn't meant for you. Simply move on. You may outgrow your teachers, or a teacher that doesn't resonate with you now may begin to resonate with you in the future as your frequency rises. Be open-minded, and let your intuition (and the Law of Attraction) lead you to what you need to know. Frequency is equivalent to knowledge. Knowledge is the doorway to expanded consciousness. Enjoy your Awakening!

The
Cardinal
Mysteries

WORKSHEETS

THE POWER OF FOCUS

What you'll need: *A timer and a natural object like a stone, crystal, or leaf.*

Overview: The purpose of most forms of meditation is energetic: to raise frequency. When you are present in the moment (being mindful) you are not focused on events of the past or future. The past and future often trigger negative thoughts, which affect frequency. The purpose of mindfulness is to be present in the moment and to be <u>neutral</u> in your emotion, to be allowing of all that you experience. This is not a state of being numb, but rather to be nonjudgmental and to observe with no expectation. Without resistant negative emotions to pull down your frequency, your frequency will rise. The *Law of Attraction* also states that we only attract in the present, so being mindful helps us know what we are attracting in the moment.

Posture: Either seated in a chair, or lotus style on a cushion, sit with your back straight. The chin slightly angles down, releasing any stress from the back of the neck. Shoulders should be aligned, not slumped or hunched forward. You should be straight and tall, with the hips, abdomen, and spine supporting you. Allow the legs and feet to relax. Let your arms rest comfortably at your sides, with your hands resting in your lap, palms facing up if you like.

Exercise: Find a stone, crystal, leaf, or other <u>pleasing</u> natural object to hold in your hand. Begin by looking at your object. Mentally note its shape, texture, size, color, and weight. Turn it over in your hand. Become familiar with all of its nuances.

Set your timer for one minute: With eyes closed, focus on the object, exploring it with your thumb, turning it over in your palm, remembering its shape, texture, size, color, and weight. Hold your focus for <u>one full minute</u> without your mind wandering. Work your way up to two minutes, then three, and so on. Have fun with it. Make it a game until you get to five minutes. Then move on to the Mindful Breathing exercise on the next page.

If working with a crystal, give it a squeeze. You may feel the **piezoelectric charge** that is released when the crystal is under pressure. See if that charge "pulses" in your hand or influences your own biofield by making you feel "buzzy."

MINDFUL BREATHING

What you'll need: *A quiet place and some time to yourself.*
Mornings are ideal, but any time is fine.

Posture: Either seated in a chair, or lotus style on a cushion, sit with your back straight. The chin gently angles down, releasing any stress from the back of the neck. Shoulders should be aligned, not slumped or hunched forward. You should be straight and tall with your diaphragm pushing down to allow for a full body breath. The hips, abdomen, and spine support you to allow for longer sitting. If you slump forward, the muscles will tire as they try to hold you up. Allow the legs and feet to relax. Let your arms rest comfortably at your sides, with your hands resting in your lap, palms facing up if you like. (You can also lie down if you can stay awake during the exercise.)

Breathing: Follow your breath, in and out through your nose. Don't try to affect the breath in any way, just let it be. Sometimes it will be shallow; other times you may sigh or take a deeper breath. After a while you will notice your breathing slowing down on its own. Focus on your breath, the sensations in your body, the feel of the air on your skin, the sounds in the room, the expansion of the ribs on the inhale, the softening of the body on the exhale. Whatever you observe is correct; there is no wrong way to do this. If your mind wanders, do not judge yourself. You are training the mind. It takes time.

Thoughts: If your mind wanders, just bring your focus back to your breath, back to the body. Breathe slowly and deeply until your body finds its own comfortable pace. Don't be bothered by your thoughts; they are normal. There is no judgment around your thoughts. Become an observer. As thoughts arise, let them go. Don't analyze or engage the mind around your stray thoughts. After 5 to 10 minutes, you may notice your mind will start to calm down. As the thoughts recede, the mind can expand. Just sit in the silence. When your thoughts return—and they will—just release them again. Focus on your breath. Notice sensations in the body.

Timer: In the beginning you can set a timer and practice for 10 minutes, building up to 20 minutes or more. You can also set an intention of duration (without a timer) and see if you naturally come out of meditation at your desired time.

TIP: You may notice that when you quiet the mind, the brain will start to remember things that need to be done and people you forgot to call or email. It can be helpful to have a notepad next to you to record these things. Then, your mind can relax knowing that you will remember when the meditation is over. Sometimes when the mind is relaxed and the chatter recedes, ideas emerge. Creative solutions arise to problems that you have been trying to solve. The notebook is also helpful for these instances. Through practice and personal discernment, you will learn the difference between typical brain-chatter and *inspired thought.*

The
Cardinal
Mysteries · A **WORKBOOK** to help you navigate your awakening.

WORKSHEET

MANTRA MEDITATION

What you'll need: *A quiet place and some time to yourself.*
Mornings are ideal, but any time is fine.

Posture: Either seated in a chair, or lotus style on a cushion, sit with your back straight. The chin gently angles down, releasing any stress from the back of the neck. Shoulders should be aligned, not slumped or hunched forward. You should be straight and tall with your diaphragm pushing down to allow for a full body breath. The hips, abdomen, and spine support you to allow for longer sitting. If you slump forward, the muscles will tire as they try to hold you up. Allow the legs and feet to relax. Let your arms rest comfortably at your sides, with your hands resting in your lap, palms facing up if you like. (You can also lie down if you can stay awake during the exercise.)

Breathing: Follow your breath, in and out through your nose. Don't try to affect the breath in any way, just let it be. Sometimes it will be shallow; other times you may sigh or take a deeper breath. After a while you will notice your breathing slowing down on its own.

Mantra: Mantras (words or phrases) are another technique to focus the mind. The mind is less likely to wander if it is occupied with a neutral thought. Quietly repeating a word or mantra to yourself gives the brain something to do; it allows the mind to rest. You may wish to research mantras; there are many to choose from, but for this exercise we will use "I Am." Repeat "I" quietly to yourself on the inhale, and "Am" on the exhale. As thoughts arise, release them and bring your focus back to the "I Am."

Practice: Build up to 20 minutes, twice a day.

Note: If meditation is challenging, remember that you can't do it wrong. There are different levels of meditation and benefits are present even with only a few minutes without the chatter. Your blood pressure comes into balance; you stimulate the parasympathetic nervous system. You create beneficial chemistry in the body like Endorphins, Serotonin, Melatonin, Human Growth Hormone, and you reduce stress hormones like Cortisol and Adrenaline. No matter how successful you feel about meditation, there is always a benefit. Over time with continued practice, your frequency will start to rise.

TIP: Throughout the day, take note of increased synchronicities, sensations in the body, repeating numbers, and anything else that you become aware of. Meditation not only affects your "inner world," it also affects your "outer world."

The **Cardinal** *Mysteries* A **WORKBOOK** to help you navigate your awakening.

WORKSHEET

ALTERNATE NOSTRIL BREATHING (NADI SHODHANA)

What you'll need: *A quiet place and 5–10 minutes.*
A great way to start a meditation, ease stress and anxiety, or aid in sleep.

Benefits: This is a great exercise to balance mind and body. Alternate nostril breathing helps focus the mind as it balances the left and right hemispheres of the brain. It helps to detoxify the body, rejuvenates the nervous system, and supports the respiratory tract.

How to: Sit up tall with a straight spine, shoulders relaxed, with an open heart. Place left hand in lap, palm up (it will not be used). The right hand is held in front of your face. Rest your index finger and middle finger between your eyebrows to act as an anchor. The thumb will rest on the right side of your nose, and the ring finger will rest on the left side of the nose. Eyes are closed.

Begin with a deep breath in and out through your nose. Close off your right nostril with your thumb.

- Inhale slowly through the left nostril (count of 4)
- Close off your left nostril with your ring finger so both nostrils are held closed (hold for 4)*
- Release the right nostril and exhale slowly (count of 4), then pause (hold for 4)
- Now inhale slowly through the right nostril (count of 4)
- Hold both nostrils closed (hold for 4)*
- Open your left nostril and release breath slowly through the left side (count of 4)
- Pause briefly at the bottom (hold for 4)

Repeat for 5 to 10 minutes. Be present in the moment and allow your mind to follow your breath.

Try to keep the inhales, holds, and exhales at a consistent length. For example, start to inhale for a count of four, hold for four, exhale for four, and hold again for four.

* If you are asthmatic or have high blood pressure, try skipping the steps where you hold the count with lungs full. <u>Breath holds with lungs empty</u> are best because they help the Carbon Dioxide level adjust, which, through the Bohr Effect, will help oxygenate the body, open airways, and dilate blood vessels.

The
Cardinal
Mysteries A **WORKBOOK** to help you navigate your awakening.

WORKSHEET

SHIFTING INTO SILENT ASKING THROUGH THE HEART

What you'll need: *A quiet place and 30–60 minutes.*
For when you want to go deeper into meditation.

Why: Perhaps you have mastered the previous exercises and you now want to go deeper. The power of prayer (asking) is in aligning with your belief. Ask while in a state of *calm expectation*, rather than fear or desperation. Sometimes our prayers are answered in the silence.

How: Find a comfortable seated position that can be maintained during the meditation.

- *State your intention. (Examples: To heal your body, to find a solution to a problem, to find a life partner, to learn to love and accept yourself, to feel peace, to send love out into the world, to bring clarity to something that you experienced, to connect with your Higher Self.)*

I ask my Guides for help and clarity, so that everything will work out for my highest good.
Today it is my intention to:

_____

- *Begin with a few minutes of Nadi Shodhana to calm your mind and become centered. Then place your hands in your lap (palms up if you like).*

- *With eyes closed, begin to breathe slowly and deeply, with equal breaths in and out through the nose. As you slip into a deeper state of relaxation, imagine that you are breathing in and out through the heart. (Studies show that focusing on the heart while mindfully breathing benefits the body more than just focusing on the breath alone.) Let your heartspace be your anchor as you allow yourself to experience whatever else arises (visual, sound, emotion, inner knowing...or just a sense of peace).*

- *If thoughts bubble up, use your "internal knowing" to determine if it is mind-chatter or inspired thought. If you think it is mind-chatter, simply release the thought and return to focusing on your breath. There is no judgment, just an awareness of the thought. But if you sense that the thought might be inspired thought, see if it expands. Draw it into your heart as you breathe. Make a mental note of it. You may even wish to end the meditation if you want to jot down an idea. Sometimes solutions come to us when the mind is clear, relaxed, and fully oxygenated as a result of breathwork.*

- *Journal or make a mental note of any synchronicities that occur during the week. Sometimes our prayers are answered in unusual ways with unlikely messengers.*

The
Cardinal
Mysteries   A **WORKBOOK** to help you navigate your awakening.

WORKSHEET

DISCOVER YOUR DIVINE BLUEPRINT (LIFE'S PURPOSE)

What you'll need: *Something to write with, a blank piece of paper, and some time to get to know yourself better.*

What: We all have a Divine Blueprint (Life's Purpose, Divine Will) and it influences our lives. If we are aligned with our Divine Blueprint, it will support us. If we are out of alignment with our Divine Blueprint, it may be holding us back from finding success in our relationships, jobs, and opportunities. This Divine Blueprint was not something assigned _to you_, it was assigned _by you_. You were intentional about what you wanted to do and what lessons you wanted to learn. If you are awakening and aware of the Shift, you may be wondering what your purpose is. You may feel that you are here for a reason and that your career is no longer a good fit. For many, the blueprint was simply to help others awaken during this time. For some it was more specific. The answer is within you; you just need to ask the right questions. The clues are in what interests you, what brings you joy and fulfillment.

Ask the following questions from the heart. Write out your answers:

1.   What do you enjoy doing, learning or reading about?
2.   Have you been interested in a certain subject all your life?
3.   If time or money were not a factor, how would you spend your days?
4.   What do you consider to be your "creative gift?"
5.   What are you good at? What comes easily to you?
6.   Are you drawn to working with children, adults, or seniors?
7.   Are you drawn to working with animals or working out in nature?
8.   Do you enjoy teaching or helping others?
9.   Do you like to help those who are sick or in need?
10. Are you a loner or a social butterfly?
11. Has a "life event" created a passion in you around a certain subject?
12. Are you passionate about a particular social issue?

These are just a few questions to get the ball rolling. The Higher Self, the part of you that has greater awareness, knows what your blueprint is. When you are interested in something, or when you feel joy, you are aligned with your Divine Will. You will not find financial success, fulfilling relationships, or an enjoyable career if you are not aligned with some aspect of your Divine Blueprint (because you are blocking your joy). Meditate on it; the answers are within you.

The *Cardinal Mysteries* A **WORKBOOK** to help you navigate your awakening.

WORKSHEET

THE POWER OF FORGIVENESS

What you'll need: *Something to write with, a blank piece of paper, and an open heart.*

Why: Forgiveness is a powerful tool to learn. Anger, hate, and revenge are lower frequencies. If we focus on being a victim, we perpetuate being a victim. If you spend years remembering someone who lied to you then you will continue to attract people who lie. Forgiveness doesn't mean that we condone what someone has done to us, but it does mean that we willingly release the negative impact that those people's actions had on us and we strive to find some meaning. Did that experience make us stronger, give us direction, give us insight as to how we made another feel in a similar experience? Sometimes the most powerful catalysts in our lives are unpleasant.

Exercise: Think of someone who hurt you then journal on the following questions:

- What emotions do you feel around this person and experience? (anger, hurt, powerlessness, self doubt, etc.) How does your body feel when you relive those memories?

- Are there any good memories? (they were fun to travel with, they got you interested in your favorite sport, they supported you in your education, etc.)

- Can you find any compassion in what they did? Could you see yourself doing the same thing to someone else? (They had anger issues they couldn't control, they were overwhelmed with being a parent, they fell in love with another, they lied to spare your feelings, they wanted to follow their joy, they felt like they were living a lie, etc.)

- Can you think of any clarity or wisdom that this situation brought you? (I'm stronger now, I am a better judge of character, I'm a better parent for it, I appreciate my current partner because of that experience, etc.)

- Can you think of any other relationships that mirror this relationship? (We often repeat our lessons if we don't learn. Look for patterns that feel familiar.)

- Does this relationship feel karmic or like it involves a pre-birth agreement (soul contract). As designers of "the game," we can stack the deck with players and conditions to act as catalysts to help us evolve.

With new insight, ask yourself again how focusing on that hurt feels. Do you notice any relief? How does your body feel now? Could you forgive them if it meant a healing for you? Could you forgive them if maybe there was a higher purpose? Forgiveness takes time so look for moments of relief and build from there. Read back over what you wrote to help with the healing process.

The
Cardinal
Mysteries A **WORKBOOK** to help you navigate your awakening.

WORKSHEET

WHAT TRIPS US UP

What you'll need: *Time to self-evaluate with an open heart.*

Why: We often look for happiness in all the wrong places. *"I'll feel successful when I get that job or salary, I'll feel fulfilled when I am married, I'll feel good about myself when I lose weight."* Sometimes we reach these goals only to find we still feel empty inside. Too often we look outside of ourselves for happiness, but happiness comes first from within. Look over the following items and ask yourself if they are tripping you up. If so, start to release lower energetic imprints by intending to shift the importance you place on these things. Releasing resistance around these subjects will help to shift your frequency.

Ask yourself if any of the following are tripping you up:

- **Materialism:** If you value "things," shift your focus from the **label** of a car, clothing, or product to the **value** they provide.

- **Time:** If you have issues around time, shift your mindset from "I never have enough time…." to affirming "I have enough time to do all that I want to do," and notice when things start to shift.

- **Monetary System:** If you have issues around abundance, notice things that trigger feelings of lack and try to shift that energy. For example, when paying a bill, find gratitude for what was provided. Affirm from a positive and truthful stance, "I love my new reliable car. I am carefree now when I drive. I appreciate being able to pay my car off over time. I have everything I need in this moment."

- **Freedom:** If you have issues around freedom, notice things that trigger those feelings. Ask yourself, "Am I allowing freedom in this moment? Is my lack of freedom real or perceived? Do I limit my own freedom to avoid conflict with another?" We often find that freedom is not as far away as we think it is.

- **Fear:** If you feel fear, ask yourself if it is <u>real fear</u> or <u>imagined fear</u>? Fear for your safety as you walk down a dark street is fear that serves you. It heightens your senses and is part of our survival mechanism. But fearing events far off in the future is always wasted energy. You're using your imagination to create a reality that you do not want. You can still be responsible and plan for the future, but if you feel fearful ask yourself if it serves you.

- **Self-Love:** Do you play the shame and blame game around your appearance or weight? Practice accepting yourself as you are, and others as they are. Your frequency will shift greatly if you practice acceptance and drop judgment.

The **Cardinal Mysteries** — A **WORKBOOK** to help you navigate your awakening.

WORKSHEET

CONNECTING TO THE HIGHER SELF

What you'll need: *A sheet of paper, scissors, and a pen.*

Why: The Higher Self is the eternal, fully conscious, most evolved part of you. It is the real YOU. It knows about all of your incarnations. It is the holder of important information. It knows the life lessons you intended to learn. It knows about your Karma. It knows the processes going on in your body. The Higher Self is connected to the Human collective, and to Universal God Source Energy. Being connected to your Higher Self helps with intuition and inner guidance. If you are among those who repeatedly see number sequences, it is the Higher Self that inspires you to look at the clock at just the right moment. The following exercise is a fun way to become more connected to your intuition through your Higher Self.

Exercise

Paper: Take a piece of letter-sized paper. Cut it in half twice, then once again so you have 8 rectangular pieces of paper. Fold each piece of paper in half. On the inside, below the fold of each sheet, write the numbers 1–7 respectively. The 8th sheet is an extra that you can throw away.

Shuffle: Shuffle the sheets so you don't see the numbers.

Quick Impression: With eyes closed select one sheet, raise it to your heart, and take a breath or two while focusing on the heart. Write down whatever word comes to mind. Don't overthink it; just write it on the top of the sheet. Under that word, write briefly what that word means to you in the moment so you can further find the context.

Repeat: Continue the process with the rest of the sheets of paper. When done you will have 7 pieces of paper with words written on top and a single number inside. Record them on page 29.

Interpret: Each number corresponds to a chakra (1=Root, 2=Sacral, 3=Solar Plexus, 4=Heart, 5=Throat, 6=Brow, 7=Crown) Interpret the words with respect to the information on the next page and develop an intention for the rest of your day.

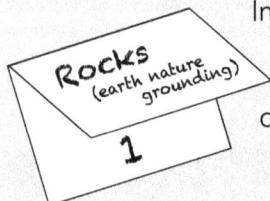

Rocks *(earth nature grounding)*

1

Extra sheet, throw away

The
Cardinal
Mysteries A **WORKBOOK** to help you navigate your awakening.

WORKSHEET

1 ROOT
Adrenals

Associated with safety, survival, grounding, and nourishment from the Earth's energy.

Examples of Health Issues: Joint pain, lower backache, constipation/elimination problems, obesity, anorexia, and poor immune system function.

2 SACRAL
Gonads (male testes & female ovaries)

Associated with desire, creativity, and sexuality.

Examples of Health Issues: Uterine or bladder problems, sexual difficulties, impotence, lack of flexibility, sciatica, lower back pain, and problems with large intestines.

3 SOLAR PLEXUS
Pancreas / Spleen

Associated with mental activities, intellect, personal power, and our personal will.

Examples of Health Issues: diabetes, hypoglycemia, gallstones, nervousness, low energy, muscle cramps, stomach problems, lumbar spine, and liver disorders.

4 HEART
Thymus

Associated with love and compassion, and our connection to the rest of humanity.

Examples of Health Issues: high blood pressure, breathing difficulties, circulation problems, shortness of breath, chest pains, disorders of the heart, and tension between the shoulders.

5 THROAT
Thyroid

Associated with self-expression, expression of truth, creativity, and communication.

Examples of Health Issues: fever, ear infections, weariness, thyroid problems, disorders in the throat, ears, voice, neck, cervical spine, hypothalamus and esophagus problems.

6 BROW
Pituitary Gland

Associated with intuition, extrasensory perception, and spiritual wisdom.

Examples of Health Issues: headaches, eye problems, pituitary and pineal gland issues, and neurological problems.

7 CROWN
Pineal Gland

Associated with enlightenment, and spiritual connection.

Examples of Health Issues: headaches, brain issues, nervous system and muscular system disorders, mental issues, and skin disorders.

WORD/ MEANING

1. Root _____	5. Throat _____
2. Sacral _____	6. Brow _____
3. Naval _____	7. Crown _____
4. Heart _____	Say or write your intention for the day (example below).

EXAMPLE

1. Root **Rocks** (earth, nature, grounding)	Today I intend to get out in nature more,
2. Sacral **Sensations** (gut feelings)	and trust my gut instincts. I will drink
3. Naval **Yellow** (Lemons, Detoxing)	lemon in my water to detox, I will practice
4. Heart **Affirmation** (I am love)	my affirmations ("I am love"), I will be
5. Throat **Love** (love what I say)	brave and love my truth as I speak it. I will
6. Brow **Elephant** (big, expansive)	continue to expand my consciousness, and
7. Crown **Bubble Gum** (fun, whimsy)	have more fun and not take life too seriously.

POWER OF THE PIVOT

What you'll need: *awareness in the moment of negative emotion.*

Why: When you think a thought that makes you feel bad, that negative emotion is trying to get your attention. It is saying, *"You're starting to attract something that you do not want."* Learning to pivot <u>in the moment</u> is a useful tool. By pivoting into a better feeling thought, you realign the energy in a more positive direction.

Exercise: Be aware in the moment of negative emotion and begin to PIVOT.

- Determine what you DON'T want (examples: I do not want to fight with this family member, I don't want to be afraid every time I pay a bill, I don't want to feel ashamed of my weight, I don't want to be alone for the rest of my life).

- Now determine what you DO want (examples: I want to have fun with my family member, I want to easily pay my bills, I want to love myself unconditionally, I want to find my life partner).

Negative emotion is a necessary part of our internal guidance system. Being aware of negative emotion allows us to PIVOT <u>in the moment</u> from what we <u>don't</u> want, to what we <u>do</u> want. Pivot by finding gentler, less specific thoughts until you go from the original negative thought to something more positive or more general. They should still feel "truthful" but you are ultimately looking for a sense of relief. For example:

- I don't want to fight with my family member. It's just an hour visit; I can get through an hour. Maybe he/she will be in a good mood today. Last visit, he/she made a nice lunch. I appreciate the effort. Maybe our visit will be okay today. It is pretty outside; maybe we can take a walk. He/she is always in a better mood when walking in nature. Maybe we will have fun today.

- I don't want to be afraid every time I pay bills. I only have to pay one bill today and I have enough. I'm expecting a few payments this week and I can pay the rest later. Business has been picking up and I can set up a payment plan for the big bill. It will be okay. I don't have to figure it all out right now. I have all that I need in the moment. I'll figure it out. It will be okay.

- Even though I feel ashamed of my weight, I am proud that I have been working on my diet and making more healthy choices. It is a process and I know that it will take time. I have many positive qualities and I am more than just my weight. So, for now, I am okay with who I am while I am *on the way* to who I want to be.

- I don't want to be alone for the rest of my life, but I know the qualities I am looking for and I'm willing to wait for the right person. Being single isn't so bad. I do enjoy more freedom than my married friends so while I am looking, I'll enjoy that freedom. The right person is out there for me, and when the time is right we will meet.

AFFIRMATIONS

What you'll need: *The intention to use a daily affirmation.*

Why: Affirmations are powerful, but often misunderstood. An affirmation that works for one person may not work for another. How does your affirmation feel? What is your level of belief? Does it feel truthful or does it feel false? Does it reinforce what you <u>want</u> or does it reinforce what you don't want? If your affirmation triggers any resistance within you, then you may be aligning energy in the opposite direction than you intended.

There are many resources that give examples of affirmations, but they all must be filtered through your belief system and emotional state.

Exercise: Read the examples below and start to develop your own affirmations.

- *How does the affirmation feel?* Say it a few times and see if any of the words trigger any resistance in you. Does it feel like a lie? Does one word "not feel right" or stand out more than the others? If so, find another word or phrase until it feels better.

  Example: "I am financially secure" may feel positively affirming for someone who is employed and looking to be more financially secure. But for someone in deep debt, it may feel like a lie. "I am aligning with Universal abundance" may feel better for now.

  Example: "I am healed" may feel positively affirming for someone whose belief is strong. But for someone in fear, "I trust my cells to know how to heal me" may feel better.

  Example: "I am divine source energy. I am love" may feel positively affirming for someone who is spiritual. But for another it may feel cloying. "I am powerful" may feel better.

- *Has your affirmation process become a mechanically thoughtless, emotionless exercise?* Affirmations work because they change our habit of thought. They re-program us to think more positively. If your affirmation has become a rote habit, it is time to change it up.

- *Dialogue.* Build momentum around your affirmation with a few minutes of affirming self-talk.

  Example: "I love being financially secure. I love being able to afford clothing that is well-made and of the finest fabrics. I love traveling and staying in lovely hotels with beautiful scenery. I love flying first class. I love being able to afford healthy organic food. I love knowing that I am a vibrational being attracting abundance to me. I love feeling abundant. I am abundant..."

- *Recognize your "call to action."* Affirmations will start to move the energy. Sometimes our prayers are answered by others, but sometimes we are the ones inspired into action. Look for inspired ideas and synchronicities; it is the Universe offering you opportunities. Act upon them.

The
Cardinal
Mysteries   A **WORKBOOK** to help you navigate your awakening.

WORKSHEET

CHECKLIST

Refer to this list to remind you of ways to shift your frequency.

☐ **Thoughts:** Your thoughts and emotions are always present. Find ways throughout your day to stay positive and heart centered. Start a gratitude journal. Feel compassion rather than judgment, hate, or fear. Becoming aware of negative thoughts and learning to pivot in the moment has the largest impact on your frequency. It is a moment-by-moment retraining of your thought process and belief system. It does not happen overnight so be easy on yourself.

☐ **Meditation & Breathwork:** When you quiet the mind, you stop resistant thought. When resistance is gone, your frequency will begin to rise. A regular meditation or mindful breathing practice (15–20 minutes, once or twice a day) will allow your frequency to naturally rise over time.

☐ **Affirmations:** Let them become a habit to change thoughts that trigger negative emotion.

☐ **Food:** Just as we have a frequency, so does the food we eat. Lighten your diet by adding more fresh fruits and vegetables (non-GMO and organic if possible, avoid chemicals). If you eat meat, consider the emotional state of the animal. A more humanely-treated animal will have a healthier frequency.

☐ **Water:** We are mostly water so our bodies need clean water at the cellular level to heal. If you can afford it, consider spring water or other forms of clean filtered water without chemicals or additives. Even tap water is asking our kidneys to do more work because they have to filter out the fluoride and chemicals that are added to kill bacteria.

☐ **Detox:** Consider detoxing if needed. Add lemon to your water; consider "greener" cleaning solvents and detergents; look for natural clothing fabrics, take Epsom salt baths—little steps make a difference.

☐ **Limit Media:** If what you are watching brings you into anger, fear, or hatred then turn it off. I realize you will want to be informed, so it is a balance that you will have to navigate.

☐ **Earth & Nature:** Earth is our home and we are tuned to her electromagnetic frequency. Do your bare feet rarely hit Mother Earth? Walk in the park or by the ocean. The Earth's charge does not easily pass through shoes so slip them off if you can and let your toes touch the grass and dirt. Find ways to bring nature inside (examples: bowls of water, indoor plants, rocks/crystals, essential oils, herbs).

☐ **Sound:** Sound has a vibrational frequency that transfers easily to the human body. Find music that feels good. Experience a crystal bowl "sound bath" at your local yoga studio. Maybe you are drawn to Gregorian Chants, Solfeggio frequencies, or other forms of sacred music.

☐ **Be Playful & Creative:** Do something creative that you love. Music, sports, art, dance, creative writing, gardening, woodworking, poetry—all joyful creative expression is beneficial.

☐ **Break Patterns:** Take a new class, meet new people, walk a different route, declutter, or rearrange furniture. Patterns hold energy that can make it harder to shift up in frequency.

☐ **Unplug:** Consider taking "Wi-Fi breaks." Reduce exposure to unnatural electromagnetic fields while you sleep by turning off your cell phone and other electronics (or place them in airplane mode if you need them nearby).